Table Of Contents

Chapter 1: The Retirement Transition

Understanding Retirement: The Shift in Lifestyle

Retirement marks a significant milestone in a man's life. After years of hard work and dedication, the time has finally come to embrace a new chapter filled with endless possibilities. However, this transition is not without its challenges. Understanding how retirement can bring about a shift in lifestyle is crucial for men over 60, especially when it comes to their mental health.

Retirement often signifies a departure from the structured routine that defined a man's working years. Suddenly, there is no longer a need to wake up early, rush to the office, and meet deadlines. This newfound freedom can be both exhilarating and overwhelming. Without the structure of work, men may find themselves feeling lost and lacking purpose. It is a crucial time to reflect and redefine what brings meaning and joy to their lives.

One of the key aspects of adjusting to retirement is recognizing the potential impact on mental health. Many men experience a sense of loss or identity crisis when they retire. The roles and responsibilities they once had may no longer exist, leaving them questioning their self-worth. It is essential to address these feelings and seek support from loved ones, friends, or professionals who can provide guidance during this transition.

Retirement offers a unique opportunity to focus on personal growth and well-being. Engaging in activities that promote mental and physical health becomes paramount. Regular exercise, pursuing hobbies, learning new skills, and engaging in social activities can help men maintain a sense of purpose and fulfillment. It is crucial to embrace the newfound freedom and explore interests that may have been neglected during working years.

Maintaining social connections is another vital aspect of mental health after retirement. Men often build strong bonds with their colleagues and may feel isolated once they leave the workforce. It is essential to nurture existing relationships and cultivate new ones. Joining clubs, volunteering, or participating in community activities can provide opportunities to connect with like-minded individuals, fostering a sense of belonging and companionship.

Lastly, embracing retirement as a time of self-discovery and personal growth is essential. Men over 60 can use this chapter to explore their passions, pursue long-held dreams, and contribute to their communities in new and meaningful ways. With the right mindset and support system, retirement can be a time of immense fulfillment and joy.

In conclusion, understanding the shift in lifestyle that retirement brings is crucial for men over 60. By addressing their mental health, embracing personal growth, maintaining social connections, and exploring new possibilities, they can navigate this transition successfully and thrive in their retirement years. It is never too late to embark on a new chapter and make the most of this exciting phase of life.

Emotions and Mental Health in Retirement

Retirement is often seen as a time of relaxation, freedom, and new opportunities. However, this significant life transition can also bring about a range of emotions and impact mental health in various ways. In this subchapter, we will explore the emotional and mental health aspects of retirement, specifically addressing the needs and concerns of men over 60.

One of the most common emotions experienced during retirement is a sense of loss. Men who have dedicated decades to their careers may find it challenging to adjust to a new routine and purpose. This loss of identity and the social interactions that came with work can lead to feelings of loneliness, isolation, and even depression. It is important for men in this age group to recognize and address these emotions, seeking support from loved ones or professional counselors.

Furthermore, retirement can also bring about financial concerns. Men who have been the primary breadwinners for their families may feel additional pressure to manage their finances effectively in retirement. Worries about money can lead to anxiety and stress, impacting mental well-being.

Seeking financial advice and creating a budget can help alleviate these concerns, allowing men to enjoy their retirement years with peace of mind.

Maintaining social connections is crucial for mental health, especially for men over 60. Retirement can sometimes lead to a shrinking social circle, as work-related friendships diminish or become less frequent. It is essential for men in this age group to actively seek out new social opportunities and engage in activities that foster connections with others. Joining community groups, volunteering, or participating in hobbies and sports can help combat feelings of isolation and improve overall well-being.

Emotional well-being can also be enhanced through self-care practices. Engaging in regular physical exercise, practicing mindfulness or meditation, and pursuing hobbies that bring joy can contribute to a positive mental state. Men over 60 should prioritize their emotional needs and explore activities that promote personal growth and fulfillment.

In conclusion, retirement is a significant life transition that can impact emotions and mental health in various ways. Men over 60 should be aware of the potential challenges they may face and take proactive steps to maintain their emotional well-being. By addressing feelings of loss, seeking financial advice, fostering social connections, and prioritizing self-care, men can navigate retirement successfully and thrive in this new chapter of their lives.

Chapter 2: Coping with Retirement

Navigating the Loss of Identity

Retirement is an inevitable milestone that men over 60 face. While it is often viewed as an opportunity to relax, travel, and enjoy the fruits of a life well-lived, it can also bring unexpected challenges, particularly when it comes to mental health. One of the most common hurdles experienced by men in this stage of life is the loss of identity.

For many years, your identity may have been closely tied to your career, your professional achievements, and the responsibilities that came with it. Suddenly, all of that changes. The regular routine, the sense of purpose, and the social interactions that once defined you may no longer be present. This can lead to a profound sense of loss and confusion, leaving you wondering, "Who am I now?"

It is crucial to recognize that this loss of identity is a normal part of the retirement transition. It is okay to feel adrift or uncertain about your place in the world. However, it is essential to actively navigate through this period to maintain good mental health and find new sources of meaning and fulfillment.

One way to begin this process is by reflecting on your passions, interests, and values. Ask yourself what brings you joy and fulfillment outside of your professional identity. Engaging in activities that align with your values, such as volunteering, pursuing hobbies, or joining community groups, can help you rebuild a sense of purpose and connection.

Additionally, seeking support from loved ones and professional resources can be immensely beneficial. Talking openly about your feelings with trusted friends or family members can provide a sense of validation and help you gain perspective. Consider joining men's mental health support groups or seeking guidance from therapists who specialize in the unique challenges faced by men over 60.

Embracing this new chapter of life requires resilience and a willingness to adapt. Remember that retirement is an opportunity for personal growth and exploration. Give yourself permission to explore new interests, take on new challenges, and redefine what success means to you. By doing so, you can not only navigate the loss of identity but also thrive after 60.

In conclusion, the loss of identity is a common struggle that many men over 60 face during retirement. However, it is not insurmountable. By reflecting on your passions, seeking support, and embracing new opportunities, you can navigate this challenging period and find renewed purpose and fulfillment in the next chapter of your life. Remember, you are not defined solely by your career, but by the multifaceted individual you have become.

Establishing a New Routine and Purpose

Retirement marks a significant transition in a man's life. After years of hard work and dedication to a career, it's time to embrace a new chapter filled with opportunities for personal growth, self-discovery, and overall well-being. However, this transition can sometimes be challenging, especially when it comes to maintaining mental health and finding a new sense of purpose. In this subchapter, we will explore the importance of establishing a new routine and purpose in your life after 60, focusing specifically on men's mental health.

One of the key factors in maintaining good mental health is having a structured routine. Retirement often disrupts the familiar daily rhythms one had during their working years. This sudden change can lead to feelings of emptiness, boredom, or even a sense of loss. Establishing a new routine is essential to provide structure and purpose to your days.

Start by setting goals and creating a schedule that incorporates activities you enjoy and find fulfilling. Engage in physical exercise to keep your body active and promote a sense of well-being. Whether it's going for a daily walk, practicing yoga, or joining a local sports club, physical activity is an excellent way to boost your mood and maintain good mental health.

Additionally, consider pursuing hobbies or interests that you may have put on hold during your working years. Whether it's painting, playing a musical instrument, gardening, or learning a new language, these activities can provide a sense of fulfillment and purpose. Engaging in hobbies not only keeps your mind active but also allows you to connect with like-minded individuals, fostering new friendships and a sense of community.

Moreover, volunteering is another meaningful way to establish a new sense of purpose. Giving back to your community or supporting causes that resonate with you can provide a sense of fulfillment and make a positive impact on others' lives. Explore local organizations or charities that align with your interests and skills, and dedicate some of your time and expertise to make a difference.

It's important to remember that establishing a new routine and purpose is a personal journey. Take the time to reflect on what truly brings you joy and fulfillment. Embrace this new chapter as an opportunity to discover new passions, invest in personal growth, and nurture your mental well-being. By doing so, you will not only adjust to retirement but also thrive after 60.

Finding Fulfillment in Hobbies and Interests

Subchapter: Finding Fulfillment in Hobbies and Interests

Introduction:
Retirement is often hailed as the golden period of one's life, a time to relax and enjoy the fruits of years of hard work. However, for many men over 60, this transition can also bring about feelings of restlessness, boredom, and a loss of purpose. In this subchapter, we will explore the importance of finding fulfillment in hobbies and

interests to address the mental health concerns that may arise during this phase of life.

The Power of Hobbies:
Engaging in hobbies and interests can be a powerful tool for men over 60 to maintain their mental well-being. Hobbies provide a sense of purpose, structure, and accomplishment, which are crucial for a healthy mindset. Whether it's gardening, woodworking, painting, or playing a musical instrument, these activities offer a creative outlet and a source of joy, boosting self-esteem and overall happiness.

Exploring New Interests:
Retirement presents an opportunity to explore new interests that may have been put on hold due to work and family commitments. It's never too late to learn something new, be it cooking, photography, or even pursuing an academic degree. Exploring new interests not only keeps the mind sharp but also introduces men to new communities and social connections, fostering a sense of belonging and fulfillment.

Physical and Mental Benefits:
Engaging in hobbies and interests can have numerous physical and mental benefits. Physical activities such as swimming, hiking, or yoga not only keep the body fit but also release endorphins, reducing stress and anxiety. Mental activities like puzzles, reading, or learning

a new language help maintain cognitive function and prevent age-related decline. By adopting a well-rounded approach to hobbies, men over 60 can enjoy both physical and mental well-being.

Building Relationships:
Hobbies and interests provide an excellent opportunity to build and strengthen relationships. Joining clubs, groups, or organizations centered around shared interests allows men to connect with like-minded individuals, fostering new friendships and a sense of camaraderie. Social interaction is vital for mental health, particularly during retirement when the social circle may shrink. Engaging in hobbies together can create lasting bonds and enrich one's overall sense of fulfillment.

Conclusion:
Retirement is a new chapter in life, and finding fulfillment in hobbies and interests is a crucial aspect of thriving after 60. By embracing new pursuits, honing existing skills, and building connections, men over 60 can experience a renewed sense of purpose, improved mental health, and a fulfilling retirement. So, let's embark on this journey together, exploring the vast array of hobbies and interests that await us in this exciting phase of life.

Chapter 3: Adjusting to a New Lifestyle

Managing Changes in Social Relationships

As men enter the golden years of their lives, they often experience significant changes in their social relationships. Retirement, while exciting, can be a challenging transition that can impact one's mental health. In this subchapter, we will explore the various aspects of managing changes in social relationships after 60 and provide valuable insights to help men thrive during this new chapter of their lives.

Retirement offers newfound freedom, but it can also bring a sense of loss and isolation. Many men find themselves disconnected from the social networks they had built over the years through work. This can lead to feelings of loneliness and affect their mental well-being. However, by proactively managing these changes, men can create a fulfilling and vibrant social life that enhances their mental health.

One crucial aspect of managing changes in social relationships is recognizing the need for support. It is essential for men over 60 to actively seek out new social connections and maintain existing ones. Engaging in activities that align with personal interests can be an excellent way to meet like-minded individuals and forge new friendships. Joining clubs, volunteering, or participating in community events can provide opportunities for social interaction and combat feelings of isolation.

Another important aspect to consider is the quality of relationships. Men should evaluate their existing friendships and assess if they are nurturing and fulfilling. It may be necessary to let go of toxic or unsupportive relationships and focus on building new relationships that bring positivity into their lives. Surrounding oneself with individuals who share similar values and interests can significantly contribute to mental well-being.

Furthermore, nurturing existing relationships is equally important. Taking the time to connect with loved ones, family, and friends can provide a strong support system during this stage of life. Regular communication, whether through phone calls, video chats, or in-person meetings, can help maintain and strengthen these relationships.

Lastly, embracing change is crucial for men over 60. It is essential to remain open to new experiences and opportunities that life may present. Stepping out of comfort zones and exploring new hobbies, interests, or even starting a new career can help men establish new social connections and maintain a sense of purpose.

In conclusion, managing changes in social relationships is a vital aspect of men's mental health after 60. By actively seeking support, evaluating and nurturing relationships, and embracing change, men can create a vibrant and fulfilling social life that enhances their overall well-being during retirement.

Exploring New Roles and Responsibilities

As men enter the new chapter of their lives after 60, adjusting to retirement can bring about a mix of emotions. While it may feel like the end of an era, it also presents an incredible opportunity for personal growth, self-discovery, and embracing new roles and responsibilities. In this subchapter, we will explore the various ways in which men over 60 can navigate this transition, specifically focusing on the important aspect of men's mental health.

Retirement often signifies a significant shift in one's daily routine and sense of purpose. Men who have dedicated their lives to their careers may find themselves at a loss when faced with the sudden absence of work-related responsibilities. This can lead to feelings of restlessness, anxiety, and even depression. However, it is essential to recognize that retirement is not the end but rather the beginning of a new chapter filled with exciting possibilities.

One way to navigate this transition successfully is by actively seeking new roles and responsibilities that align with personal interests and passions. Whether it's pursuing a long-lost hobby, volunteering for a cause close to your heart, or even starting a small business venture, finding meaningful activities can provide a sense of purpose and fulfillment. Engaging in such activities not only contributes to personal growth but also positively impacts mental health and overall well-being.

Moreover, men over 60 can explore new roles within their families and communities. Becoming a mentor, a supportive partner, or a trusted confidant can foster stronger relationships and deepen connections with loved ones.

Taking on responsibilities within community organizations, such as serving on boards or leading initiatives, allows men to contribute their skills and experiences to make a meaningful impact on society.

In the context of men's mental health, it is crucial to acknowledge and address any emotional challenges that may arise during this transition. Seeking support from friends, family, or professional therapists can provide a safe space to talk about concerns, fears, and hopes for the future. Engaging in regular physical exercise, maintaining a balanced diet, and practicing mindfulness techniques can also contribute to overall mental well-being.

In conclusion, exploring new roles and responsibilities is an integral part of adjusting to retirement for men over 60. By actively seeking meaningful activities, embracing new opportunities, and prioritizing mental health, men can thrive in this new chapter of their lives. Remember, retirement is not the end; it is a chance for personal growth, self-discovery, and finding renewed purpose.

Financial Considerations and Budgeting

One of the crucial aspects of adjusting to retirement and thriving after 60 is ensuring that your financial well-being is secure. As men over 60, it is essential to understand the financial considerations and implement effective budgeting strategies to maintain a stable and stress-free retirement.

Retirement brings about a significant change in financial circumstances, as the income stream from employment ceases. It is imperative to carefully evaluate your financial situation, taking into account factors such as savings, investments, and any pensions or retirement plans you may have. Assessing your current financial state will provide a foundation upon which you can build a sustainable budgeting plan.

Creating a realistic budget is essential to effectively manage your finances during retirement. Start by identifying your essential expenses, including housing, utilities, healthcare, and transportation costs. Next, consider discretionary expenses such as entertainment, travel, and hobbies. By categorizing your expenses, you can allocate your income accordingly and prioritize your financial needs.

In addition to budgeting, careful consideration of long-term financial goals is crucial. As men over 60, it is essential to plan for unforeseen circumstances, such as medical emergencies or the need for long-term care. Exploring insurance options, such as health insurance and long-term care insurance, can provide peace of mind and protect your savings from unexpected expenses.

It is also essential to stay informed about investment opportunities and strategies that can help grow your wealth during retirement. Seeking the advice of a financial advisor can be beneficial in navigating the complexities of investment options and ensuring that your portfolio is diversified and aligned with your risk tolerance.

Furthermore, maintaining an active and healthy lifestyle can positively impact your mental health and financial well-being.

Engaging in physical activities and hobbies not only provide enjoyment but can also reduce healthcare costs in the long run. Additionally, taking care of your mental health through activities like meditation, socializing, and pursuing new interests can enhance your overall well-being and positively influence your financial decisions.

In conclusion, as men over 60, financial considerations and budgeting are essential components of adjusting to retirement and thriving in this new chapter of life. Evaluating your financial situation, creating a realistic budget, planning for long-term goals, and staying informed about investment opportunities will help ensure financial stability. Moreover, taking care of your mental and physical health will contribute to a fulfilling retirement experience. By implementing these strategies, you can embrace retirement with confidence, knowing that your financial future is secure.

Chapter 4: Mental Health After 60

Recognizing and Addressing Depression and Anxiety

Recognizing and Addressing Depression and Anxiety: Men's Mental Health After 60

Introduction:

In this subchapter, we will delve into the crucial topic of recognizing and addressing depression and anxiety among men over 60. Retirement is often considered a time of relaxation and fulfillment, but it can also bring its own set of challenges. Mental health concerns, such as depression and anxiety, can affect individuals during this transitional phase. By understanding the signs, seeking help, and adopting coping strategies, men over 60 can effectively navigate these challenges and thrive in their new chapter of life.

Recognizing the Signs:

Depression and anxiety can manifest in different ways for individuals, and recognizing the signs is the first step toward addressing these mental health concerns. Some common signs of depression may include prolonged sadness, loss of interest in previously enjoyed activities, changes in appetite or sleep patterns, persistent fatigue, and difficulty concentrating. Anxiety, on the other hand, often presents as excessive worry, restlessness, irritability, and physical symptoms like headaches or a racing heart.

Seeking Help:

Acknowledging one's mental health struggles and seeking help is crucial. Men over 60 may be more hesitant to reach out due to societal expectations or a fear of being perceived as weak. However, it is important to remember that seeking help is a sign of strength. There are several avenues available to address mental health concerns, including therapy, support groups, and even online resources. By reaching out to professionals or talking to trusted friends and family members, men over 60 can find the support they need to overcome these challenges.

Coping Strategies:

In addition to seeking professional help, implementing coping strategies can significantly improve mental well-being. Engaging in regular physical exercise, maintaining a healthy diet, and getting enough sleep are essential for overall mental health. Engaging in hobbies, joining social groups, and staying connected with friends and loved ones can also combat feelings of isolation and loneliness. Mindfulness techniques, such as meditation or deep breathing exercises, can help manage anxiety and promote self-awareness.

Conclusion:

As men embark on their retirement journey, it is crucial to prioritize mental health. Recognizing the signs of depression and anxiety, seeking help, and implementing coping strategies are vital steps toward thriving after 60. By addressing these mental health concerns head-on, men can embrace their new chapter with resilience, happiness, and a renewed sense of purpose.

Remember, it is never too late to prioritize your mental well-being and create a fulfilling and rewarding retirement experience.

Dealing with Loneliness and Isolation

As we enter the new chapter of retirement, many of us men over 60 may experience a sense of loneliness or isolation. After years of being surrounded by colleagues, friends, and a structured routine, the sudden shift can leave us feeling adrift and disconnected. However, it is essential to recognize that we are not alone in this struggle, and there are ways to overcome these feelings and thrive in our golden years.

Loneliness and isolation can have a significant impact on our mental health after 60. Studies have shown that prolonged periods of loneliness can lead to increased rates of depression, anxiety, and even cognitive decline. Therefore, it is crucial to address these feelings head-on and take steps to reconnect with the world around us.

One effective strategy is to establish a strong support network. Reach out to old friends, family members, or even join local clubs or organizations that cater to your interests. Building new connections can help combat feelings of isolation and provide a sense of belonging. Engaging in regular social activities and maintaining a busy schedule can also help combat loneliness.

Technology can also be a valuable tool in combating isolation. Embrace the digital world and use it to your advantage. Connect with loved ones through video calls or join online communities tailored to your hobbies or passions. Whether it's a virtual book club or a discussion forum, these online platforms can provide an avenue for social interaction and intellectual stimulation.

Volunteering can also be a rewarding way to combat loneliness and isolation while giving back to the community. By engaging in meaningful activities, we can regain a sense of purpose and fulfillment. Whether it's mentoring younger individuals or participating in local charity events, volunteering can help us connect with others and make a positive impact.

Lastly, it is essential to prioritize self-care and mental well-being. Engage in activities that bring you joy and promote a sense of inner peace. This could include hobbies, exercise, meditation, or even seeking professional help through therapy or support groups. Taking care of ourselves mentally and physically is vital for overall happiness and contentment.

In conclusion, the transition into retirement can sometimes bring forth feelings of loneliness and isolation for men over 60. However, by establishing a support network, utilizing technology, volunteering, and prioritizing self-care, we can navigate this new chapter with confidence and thrive in our golden years. Remember, you are not alone, and there are resources and strategies available to help you reconnect and find fulfillment in this exciting phase of life.

Seeking Support and Professional Help

In the journey through retirement, it's essential for men over 60 to pay attention to their mental health and seek the necessary support and professional help when needed. This subchapter aims to shed light on the importance of addressing and maintaining men's mental well-being during this new phase of life.

Retirement is often hailed as a time of relaxation, freedom, and enjoyment. However, it can also bring about significant changes that may impact mental health. The loss of daily routines, social connections, and a sense of purpose can lead to feelings of loneliness, anxiety, and even depression. Recognizing these potential challenges is the first step towards seeking the support and professional help that can make a real difference.

One of the most crucial aspects of seeking support is breaking the stigma surrounding men's mental health. Society has long perpetuated the notion that men should be strong, independent, and self-reliant. As a result, many men find it challenging to admit when they are struggling emotionally. However, it's important to understand that seeking help is not a sign of weakness, but rather an act of strength and self-care.

There are various avenues for seeking support and professional help. One option is to reach out to trusted friends or family members who can offer a listening ear and emotional support. Sharing your thoughts and feelings with someone who understands can provide a sense of relief and reassurance.

Additionally, consider speaking with a mental health professional who specializes in men's mental health after 60. These professionals can offer valuable insights, coping strategies, and personalized treatment plans tailored to your specific needs. They can help you navigate the challenges that retirement may present and provide guidance on maintaining a healthy mindset.

Support groups specifically targeted towards men over 60 can also prove immensely helpful. Engaging with individuals who are experiencing similar struggles can foster a sense of camaraderie and provide a safe space for open discussions. These groups can be found both in-person and online, offering flexibility and accessibility.

Remember, seeking support and professional help is not a sign of weakness but a proactive step towards maintaining and improving your mental well-being. By taking this important step, men over 60 can not only adjust to retirement but also thrive during this new chapter of life.

Chapter 5: Aging and Independence

Maintaining Physical Health and Mobility

As men enter their retirement years, it becomes increasingly important to prioritize their physical health and mobility. This subchapter delves into the various aspects of physical well-being and offers practical tips and advice to help men over 60 maintain an active and fulfilling lifestyle.

Physical health plays a crucial role in overall well-being, and it is never too late to start making positive changes. Regular exercise is key to maintaining strength, flexibility, and cardiovascular health. Engaging in activities such as walking, swimming, or cycling can help improve endurance and keep weight in check. Additionally, strength training exercises can help combat muscle loss and maintain bone density, reducing the risk of fractures.

However, it is essential to consult with a healthcare professional before embarking on a new exercise regimen. They can provide guidance on the most suitable activities and offer advice on any potential limitations or precautions to be aware of.

In addition to exercise, proper nutrition is vital for men over 60. A well-balanced diet rich in fruits, vegetables, lean proteins, and whole grains can help prevent chronic diseases and boost energy levels. It is important to stay hydrated by drinking plenty of water throughout the day and limit the consumption of processed foods high in salt, sugar, and unhealthy fats.

Furthermore, maintaining mobility is crucial for independent living and overall quality of life. Regular stretching and flexibility exercises can help improve mobility and reduce the risk of injury. Incorporating activities like yoga or tai chi can enhance balance, coordination, and promote relaxation.

Mental health is closely intertwined with physical well-being. Retirement can bring about significant life changes and transitions, which may impact mental health. It is essential for men over 60 to pay attention to their mental well-being and seek support if needed. Engaging in social activities, pursuing hobbies, and staying connected with loved ones can help combat feelings of loneliness and isolation.

In conclusion, this subchapter emphasizes the importance of maintaining physical health and mobility for men over 60. By prioritizing regular exercise, proper nutrition, and seeking support for mental health, men can thrive during their retirement years.

Taking care of oneself physically and mentally allows for the pursuit of new interests, continued independence, and an overall sense of well-being.

Adapting to Changes in Cognitive Abilities

As men age, it is natural for cognitive abilities to undergo certain changes. While some of these changes may be subtle, others can be more pronounced and may impact daily life. Adapting to these changes in cognitive abilities becomes crucial in maintaining mental health and overall wellbeing after the age of 60.

One common cognitive change that men may experience as they get older is a decline in processing speed. Tasks that used to be completed effortlessly may now take longer. This can be frustrating and may lead to feelings of incompetence or even anxiety. However, it is important to remember that this decline is a normal part of the aging process and does not necessarily indicate a decline in intelligence or capability.

Another cognitive change that often occurs with age is a decrease in working memory. This can make it more challenging to retain and recall information, leading to forgetfulness or difficulty multitasking. To adapt to these changes, it can be helpful to develop strategies such as using memory aids like calendars or notes, breaking tasks into smaller steps, or practicing mindfulness techniques to improve focus and concentration.

Additionally, language skills may be affected by cognitive changes. Men may find it harder to find the right words or to express themselves clearly. This can impact communication and social interactions, potentially leading to feelings of isolation or frustration. Engaging in activities that stimulate language skills, such as reading, writing, or engaging in meaningful conversations, can be beneficial in maintaining these abilities.

Adapting to changes in cognitive abilities also involves taking care of one's physical health. Regular exercise, a balanced diet, and adequate sleep are all essential components of maintaining cognitive function. Staying socially active and engaged in meaningful activities can also help stimulate the brain and prevent cognitive decline.

It is important for men over 60 to be proactive in addressing these changes and seeking support when needed. Discussing concerns with healthcare professionals, participating in cognitive training programs, or joining support groups for men's mental health can all be valuable resources.

Remember, adapting to changes in cognitive abilities is a natural part of the aging process. By understanding these changes and taking proactive steps to maintain mental health, men over 60 can continue to thrive and enjoy a fulfilling retirement.

Making Housing and Lifestyle Adjustments

As men reach the age of 60, they often find themselves at a crossroads in life. Retirement has arrived, bringing with it a newfound freedom and a chance to explore new opportunities. However, this stage also requires some adjustments, particularly when it comes to housing and lifestyle choices. In this subchapter, we will discuss the importance of making these adjustments and provide practical advice for men over 60.

One aspect to consider is downsizing. As children grow up and move out, maintaining a large family home may no longer be necessary. Downsizing to a smaller, more manageable space can not only reduce the burden of maintenance but also free up resources for other activities. It is essential to carefully evaluate your needs and desires to find a home that suits your lifestyle and budget.

Furthermore, it is important to assess your current living situation and determine if any modifications are required to support your evolving needs. Aging can bring physical limitations, so it may be necessary to make your home more accessible and safe. Installing handrails, ramps, or even considering a move to a single-story dwelling can greatly enhance your quality of life.

Apart from housing adjustments, lifestyle changes are also crucial in maintaining good mental health after 60. Retirement can be a significant life transition, and some men may struggle with a sense of purpose or identity. Engaging in hobbies, volunteering, or pursuing new interests can provide a renewed sense of meaning and fulfillment.

Additionally, staying socially connected is vital for mental well-being. Building and maintaining strong relationships with family, friends, and community members can combat feelings of isolation. Joining clubs or groups centered around shared interests can help forge new connections and foster a sense of belonging.

Lastly, caring for one's physical health is paramount for mental well-being. Engaging in regular exercise, eating a balanced diet, and getting enough sleep are all crucial components of a healthy lifestyle. By taking care of your physical health, you are better equipped to face the challenges and joys of retirement.

In conclusion, making housing and lifestyle adjustments is an essential part of thriving after the age of 60. Downsizing, modifying your living space, exploring new hobbies, nurturing relationships, and prioritizing physical health are all key components to consider. By embracing these adjustments, men over 60 can create a fulfilling and purposeful retirement, leading to improved mental well-being and overall happiness.

Chapter 6: Relationships and Intimacy

Nurturing Friendships and Building New Connections

As men enter the new chapter of retirement, it is crucial to recognize the importance of nurturing friendships and building new connections. Often, the focus on career and family responsibilities can cause friendships to take a backseat, leaving many men feeling isolated and lonely as they enter their senior years. However, maintaining strong social connections is essential for men's mental health after 60.

Friendships play a vital role in our lives, providing support, companionship, and a sense of belonging. Research has shown that individuals with strong social networks tend to have lower rates of depression, anxiety, and cognitive decline. By investing time and effort into nurturing existing friendships and cultivating new ones, men can significantly improve their overall well-being.

One way to nurture friendships is by actively staying in touch with old friends. Retirement offers an ideal opportunity to reconnect with long-lost buddies from different phases of life. Whether it's organizing regular meet-ups, phone calls, or even joining social media platforms to stay updated, these efforts can help rekindle old connections and foster a sense of camaraderie.

Additionally, building new connections is equally important. Retirement opens doors to a plethora of opportunities to meet like-minded individuals. Joining community clubs, volunteering for local organizations, or taking part in hobby groups can be fantastic ways to find new friends who share similar interests. Engaging in activities that bring joy and fulfillment not only helps to build connections but also promotes a sense of purpose and self-worth.

Furthermore, it's essential to recognize that building new friendships after 60 may require stepping out of one's comfort zone. Taking the initiative to attend social events or strike up conversations with strangers can be intimidating, but it can lead to rewarding connections. By adopting a positive and open mindset, men can embrace new experiences and expand their social circles.

In conclusion, nurturing friendships and building new connections is vital for men's mental health after 60. As retirement brings about a shift in priorities, it is crucial to invest time and effort into maintaining existing friendships and actively seeking new connections. By fostering meaningful relationships, men can enhance their overall well-being, combat feelings of loneliness, and enjoy a fulfilling and thriving retirement. Remember, it's never too late to make new friends and strengthen existing bonds.

Communication and Emotional Intimacy with Partners

In our journey through life, relationships play a crucial role in our overall well-being and happiness. As we enter the golden years of retirement, maintaining strong connections and emotional intimacy with our partners becomes even more important.

This subchapter explores the significance of communication and emotional intimacy for men over 60, focusing on their mental health and overall well-being.

Retirement brings about a significant change in our daily routines, and it is essential to navigate this transition together with our partners. Effective communication becomes the cornerstone of a successful relationship during this phase. Open and honest communication allows both partners to express their needs, desires, and fears, fostering a deeper understanding and connection. It is crucial to actively listen to our partners, providing them with a safe space to share their thoughts and emotions.

Emotional intimacy, often overlooked or undervalued, becomes a vital component of a fulfilling relationship after 60. It involves sharing our deepest emotions, vulnerabilities, and dreams with our partners. This level of intimacy creates a sense of trust and can enhance the overall mental well-being of men in this age group. Emotional intimacy requires effort and a willingness to be vulnerable, but the rewards are immeasurable.

To foster emotional intimacy, it is important to prioritize quality time together. Engaging in activities that bring joy and create shared memories can strengthen the emotional bond. Whether it's going for walks, traveling, or pursuing common hobbies, these shared experiences can deepen the connection between partners.

Moreover, communication and emotional intimacy can positively impact men's mental health after 60. Engaging in open and honest conversations with our partners can alleviate feelings of loneliness, anxiety, and depression. It provides an outlet to discuss any challenges or concerns related to retirement, health, or aging. By sharing these burdens with a trusted partner, the weight becomes more manageable, and a sense of support and understanding is cultivated.

In conclusion, as men over 60 embark on this new chapter of their lives, prioritizing communication and emotional intimacy with their partners is crucial for their mental health and overall well-being. By actively engaging in open and honest conversations, creating shared experiences, and fostering emotional intimacy, men can thrive in their relationships and enjoy a fulfilling retirement. Remember, it is never too late to strengthen the bond with your partner and create a foundation of love, trust, and understanding that will last a lifetime.

Exploring Dating and Romantic Relationships

In this subchapter, we delve into the exciting world of dating and romantic relationships for men over 60. While retirement may mark the end of one chapter, it also presents an opportunity for a fresh beginning in this aspect of life. As we age, our emotional needs evolve, and it is important to understand how to navigate these changes while maintaining mental well-being.

Dating after 60 can be a transformative experience, providing a chance to forge meaningful connections and rediscover oneself. However, it is essential to approach this new phase with a positive mindset and a commitment to self-care. Men's mental health after 60 is of utmost importance, and exploring dating and romantic relationships can contribute significantly to overall well-being.

One crucial aspect to consider is self-reflection. Take the time to assess your own desires, values, and expectations from a relationship. This introspection will help you identify the qualities you seek in a partner and establish meaningful connections based on mutual understanding and respect.

Additionally, it is essential to embrace the changes that come with age and adjust your approach to dating accordingly. Recognize that physical appearances may have changed, but wisdom and life experiences have enriched your character. Focus on highlighting your strengths, such as your sense of humor, intelligence, or compassion. Confidence in oneself is attractive at any age.

Technology has revolutionized the dating landscape, and men over 60 should embrace these advancements. Online dating platforms provide an excellent opportunity to connect with like-minded individuals. However, it is crucial to exercise caution and prioritize safety when engaging with potential partners online.

Remember, dating after 60 is not solely about finding a romantic partner but also about cultivating a vibrant social life. Engage in activities and hobbies that interest you, join clubs or organizations, and attend community events. By expanding your social circle, you increase your chances of meeting someone with shared interests and values.

Lastly, do not hesitate to seek support and guidance when needed. Surround yourself with friends and family who will support you throughout this journey. Professional therapists or counselors specializing in men's mental health can also provide valuable advice and assistance in navigating the complexities of dating and relationships.

In conclusion, exploring dating and romantic relationships after 60 can be a fulfilling and enriching experience. By approaching this new chapter with an open mind, embracing change, and prioritizing self-care, men over 60 can establish meaningful connections and thrive in their personal lives while maintaining their mental well-being.

Chapter 7: Self-Care and Wellness

Prioritizing Physical Well-being

As men over the age of 60, it is essential to recognize the importance of prioritizing your physical well-being. This chapter aims to shed light on the significance of maintaining good physical health, not only for your overall well-being but also for your mental health.

Physical well-being plays a crucial role in our lives, especially as we age. It is a cornerstone of a fulfilling retirement and thriving in our golden years. Engaging in regular physical activity can have a profound impact on our mental health, reducing the risks of depression, anxiety, and cognitive decline.

One of the key aspects of prioritizing physical well-being is staying active. This does not mean you have to run marathons or engage in intense workouts. Instead, find activities that you enjoy and that suit your fitness level. It could be as simple as taking daily walks, practicing yoga, swimming, or even gardening. Regular exercise not only improves physical strength and flexibility but also releases endorphins, which boost mood and overall mental well-being.

Another crucial factor in maintaining physical well-being is adopting a healthy and balanced diet. As we age, our bodies require specific nutrients to support optimal health. Focus on consuming a variety of fruits, vegetables, whole grains, lean proteins, and healthy fats.

Avoid excessive salt, sugar, and processed foods, as they can contribute to various health issues. A well-nourished body will not only have more energy but also provide the necessary fuel for a sharp mind.

Furthermore, it is important to prioritize regular medical check-ups and screenings. As men over 60, certain health conditions become more prevalent, such as heart disease, diabetes, and prostate cancer. Regular check-ups allow for early detection and intervention, increasing the chances of successful treatment and improved outcomes.

Lastly, maintaining a healthy social life is vital for your physical and mental well-being. Engage in activities that foster social connections, such as joining clubs, volunteering, or participating in group exercises. Social interactions can provide a sense of purpose, reduce feelings of loneliness, and contribute to overall happiness.

Prioritizing your physical well-being after the age of 60 is a lifelong commitment. By engaging in regular physical activity, eating a balanced diet, attending regular check-ups, and nurturing your social life, you can enjoy a fulfilling retirement and thrive mentally as you embark on this new chapter of your life. Remember, it is never too late to start prioritizing your physical well-being – your body and mind will thank you for it.

Enhancing Mental and Emotional Resilience

As men enter their 60s and embark on the journey of retirement, it is essential to prioritize mental and emotional well-being. This subchapter explores the importance of enhancing mental and emotional resilience during this phase of life. Retirement can bring both excitement and uncertainty, and maintaining good mental health becomes crucial in navigating this new chapter successfully.

One key aspect of enhancing mental and emotional resilience is embracing change. Retirement represents a significant life transition, and it is essential to acknowledge and embrace the changes that come with it. By adopting a positive mindset and viewing retirement as an opportunity for personal growth and exploration, men can approach this phase with optimism and resilience.

Staying socially connected is another vital aspect of mental and emotional well-being after 60. Building and maintaining strong relationships with friends, family, and the wider community can provide a support system during this transitional period. Engaging in social activities, joining clubs or organizations, or even volunteering can help foster a sense of purpose and belonging, thus reducing the risk of isolation and loneliness.

Prioritizing self-care is equally important for men's mental health after 60. This includes taking care of physical health through regular exercise, a balanced diet, and sufficient sleep. Engaging in activities that bring joy and fulfillment, such as pursuing hobbies or learning new skills, can also contribute to a sense of well-being.

Moreover, seeking professional help should never be underestimated. Men should not hesitate to reach out to mental health professionals or support groups if they are struggling with their mental and emotional well-being. Therapy or counseling sessions can provide valuable tools and strategies to cope with any challenges that retirement may bring.

Lastly, maintaining a positive outlook on life is crucial for mental and emotional resilience. Practicing gratitude, mindfulness, and self-reflection can help men cultivate a sense of contentment and appreciation for the present moment. By focusing on the positive aspects of retirement and embracing the opportunities it presents, men can navigate this phase with resilience and thrive in their new chapter.

In conclusion, enhancing mental and emotional resilience is paramount for men over 60 as they adjust to retirement and strive for a fulfilling life. By embracing change, staying socially connected, prioritizing self-care, seeking professional help when needed, and adopting a positive mindset, men can enhance their mental and emotional well-being during this transformative period.

Incorporating Healthy Habits into Daily Life

Taking care of one's physical and mental health becomes increasingly important as we age, especially for men over 60. In this subchapter, we will explore the significance of incorporating healthy habits into daily life and how they can positively impact men's mental health during their retirement years.

Regular exercise is a cornerstone of maintaining good health. Engaging in physical activities not only keeps the body fit but also has numerous mental health benefits. Whether it's going for a brisk walk, cycling, swimming, or joining a fitness class, finding an activity that suits your interests and abilities is key. Exercise releases endorphins, the "feel-good" hormones, which can alleviate stress, anxiety, and depression. It also promotes better sleep, boosts self-confidence, and improves cognitive function, helping men maintain their mental sharpness.

Alongside exercise, incorporating a balanced diet into your daily routine is essential. Opting for a variety of nutrient-rich foods such as fruits, vegetables, whole grains, lean proteins, and healthy fats can help prevent chronic diseases and maintain a healthy weight. Additionally, certain foods like fatty fish, nuts, and seeds are rich in omega-3 fatty acids, which are known to support brain health and reduce the risk of cognitive decline. Prioritizing hydration by drinking plenty of water throughout the day is also crucial for overall well-being.

Another healthy habit to consider is maintaining social connections. Retirement can sometimes lead to feelings of isolation and loneliness, which can have a negative impact on mental health. Engaging in social activities, joining community groups or clubs, and staying connected with friends and family can combat these feelings. Regular social interactions provide opportunities for laughter, emotional support, and a sense of belonging, all of which contribute to improved mental well-being.

Lastly, incorporating mindfulness practices, such as meditation or deep breathing exercises, into daily life can help manage stress and promote relaxation. These practices can be particularly beneficial for men over 60, as they may be facing new challenges and transitions during their retirement. Mindfulness allows individuals to focus on the present moment, cultivate gratitude, and reduce negative thoughts or worries.

By incorporating these healthy habits into daily life, men over 60 can prioritize their mental health and well-being during retirement. Whether it's through exercise, a balanced diet, social connections, or mindfulness practices, taking care of oneself holistically is paramount. Embracing these habits can lead to a fulfilling and thriving retirement, allowing men to fully enjoy this new chapter of their lives.

Chapter 8: Meaning and Legacy

Reflecting on Life Experiences and Wisdom

As men reach the milestone age of 60 and enter retirement, they often find themselves with a newfound abundance of time and a wealth of life experiences to reflect upon. This subchapter aims to delve into the importance of introspection and self-reflection during this stage of life, emphasizing the impact it can have on men's mental health and overall well-being.

One of the greatest benefits of reaching this stage is the wisdom that comes with a lifetime of experiences. Reflecting on these experiences allows men to gain a deeper understanding of themselves and the world around them. It provides an opportunity to appreciate the lessons learned, the mistakes made, and the growth that has occurred throughout their lives. By taking the time to reflect, men can gain a sense of fulfillment and purpose, as well as a renewed perspective on life.

Self-reflection also plays a crucial role in maintaining good mental health after 60. Retirement can bring about significant changes and challenges, including a loss of identity and a shift in social circles. It is during this time that men may find themselves questioning their purpose and direction in life. By engaging in introspection, they can navigate this transition more effectively, finding new passions and interests, and redefining their sense of self.

Furthermore, reflecting on life experiences and wisdom allows men to pass down valuable knowledge to younger generations. Sharing stories and lessons learned can be incredibly fulfilling, not only for the person recounting them but also for the individuals who benefit from their wisdom. It fosters a sense of legacy, ensuring that their experiences and insights continue to impact others long after they are gone.

In this subchapter, we will explore various techniques and exercises to facilitate self-reflection. We will encourage men over 60 to carve out dedicated time for introspection, whether through journaling, meditation, or engaging in meaningful conversations with loved ones.

By providing practical tools and insights, we hope to assist men in their journey of self-discovery and personal growth during this transformative stage of life.

In conclusion, reflecting on life experiences and wisdom is a vital component of men's mental health after 60. By embracing self-reflection, men can gain a deeper understanding of themselves, find fulfillment in their accomplishments, and navigate the challenges that retirement brings. Moreover, this process allows them to leave a meaningful legacy and pass down their wisdom to future generations.

Through this subchapter, we aim to inspire and empower men over 60 to embark on a journey of self-reflection and thrive in this new chapter of their lives.

Leaving a Lasting Impact on Future Generations

As men over 60, we have reached a stage in life where we can reflect on our past accomplishments, but also look towards the future and consider the legacy we want to leave behind. One of the most profound ways to make a lasting impact is by nurturing the mental health and well-being of future generations. In this subchapter, we will explore the importance of men's mental health after 60 and how we can contribute to a thriving and resilient society.

The transition into retirement can sometimes be challenging, as it brings with it a shift in identity and a change in daily routine. It is crucial to prioritize our mental health during this phase of life. By taking care of ourselves, we set an example for younger generations to prioritize their own well-being. Engaging in activities that bring us joy, maintaining social connections, and seeking professional help if needed are all essential steps towards maintaining good mental health.

In addition to self-care, it is vital to consider how we can support the mental health of those around us, particularly our children, grandchildren, and even great-grandchildren. By being open and honest about our own mental health struggles, we reduce the stigma surrounding mental health and create a safe space for younger generations to seek help when needed. Sharing our experiences and offering guidance can provide a valuable source of support and inspiration for those who may be facing similar challenges.

Furthermore, we can actively contribute to the mental health of future generations by getting involved in community organizations, volunteering, or mentoring programs. By sharing our wisdom and life experiences, we can guide and inspire young individuals, helping them navigate the complexities of life and fostering their mental well-being. Our unique perspectives and lessons learned can be invaluable resources for the next generation.

Leaving a lasting impact on future generations goes beyond our own family. By advocating for mental health awareness and supporting initiatives that prioritize mental well-being, we can create a society that values and nurtures the mental health of all its members. Whether it is through supporting legislation for mental health resources or participating in community events, our contributions can shape a brighter future.

In conclusion, as men over 60, we have the power to leave a lasting impact on future generations by prioritizing our own mental health, supporting the mental health of those around us, and advocating for mental well-being on a broader scale. By taking these steps, we can contribute to a society that is resilient, compassionate, and thriving. Let us embrace this new chapter in our lives and make a difference that will be felt for generations to come.

Finding Meaning and Purpose in Later Life

Subchapter: Finding Meaning and Purpose in Later Life

Introduction:

As men enter their 60s and beyond, a new chapter begins, a phase filled with opportunities for personal growth, self-discovery, and finding renewed purpose. Retirement can be a time of great joy and fulfillment, but it can also bring about challenges to one's mental health. In this subchapter, we will explore the importance of finding meaning and purpose in later life and how it contributes to men's mental well-being after 60.

Rediscovering Your Passions:

Retirement offers a unique chance to reconnect with your passions and interests. Take the time to reflect on what truly brings you joy and fulfillment. Whether it's exploring new hobbies, traveling, volunteering, or delving into creative pursuits, engaging in activities that align with your values and interests can provide a sense of purpose and contribute positively to your mental health.

Reconnecting with Loved Ones:

Later life presents an excellent opportunity to strengthen relationships with loved ones. Take the time to build deeper connections with your family, friends, and community. Engaging in meaningful conversations, sharing experiences, and participating in activities together can provide a sense of belonging and purpose. Research shows that strong social connections are crucial for mental well-being, especially in older adults.

Contributing to Society:
Many men find a sense of purpose and fulfillment by giving back to their communities. Consider volunteering for a cause that resonates with you. Whether it's mentoring younger generations, helping out at a local charity, or sharing your expertise through teaching or coaching, making a difference in the lives of others can bring immense satisfaction and meaning to your own life.

Continued Learning and Growth:
Learning is a lifelong journey, and retirement provides an excellent opportunity to explore new interests and expand your knowledge. Engaging in intellectual activities, attending workshops, taking up new courses, or even pursuing a degree can help you stay mentally sharp, boost your self-confidence, and instill a sense of purpose.

Embracing Personal Growth:
Later life is a time to reflect on your life's achievements and experiences. Embrace personal growth by setting new goals, challenging yourself, and embracing change. By continually

evolving and striving for self-improvement, you can find meaning and purpose in your day-to-day life.

Conclusion:
Finding meaning and purpose in later life is essential for men over 60 to maintain their mental well-being. By rediscovering passions, strengthening relationships, contributing to society, pursuing continued learning, and embracing personal growth, you can thrive in this new chapter of your life. Remember, it is never too late to find meaning and purpose; the possibilities are endless, and the journey ahead is filled with opportunities for fulfillment and joy.

Chapter 9: Navigating Healthcare and Age-Related Challenges

Managing Chronic Illnesses and Health Conditions

As men enter their retirement years and reach the age of 60 and beyond, it is crucial to prioritize their well-being, both physically and mentally. Chronic illnesses and health conditions can often become more prevalent during this stage of life, requiring proactive management and care. In this subchapter, we will explore some essential strategies for effectively managing these health challenges, with a specific focus on men's mental health after 60.

One of the most critical aspects of managing chronic illnesses and health conditions is to establish a strong support network. It is essential to surround oneself with individuals who understand the unique challenges faced by men in this age group. Whether it be friends, family members, or support groups, having a reliable support system can make a significant difference in managing chronic illnesses. These individuals can provide emotional support, offer practical advice, and share their own experiences, creating a sense of camaraderie and understanding.

Additionally, seeking professional help is crucial for men over 60 dealing with chronic illnesses. Consulting with healthcare providers who specialize in geriatric care can ensure that their specific needs are addressed and managed appropriately. Mental health professionals play a vital role in helping men navigate the emotional aspects of living with a chronic illness. They can offer coping strategies, provide guidance on maintaining a positive mindset, and assist in developing effective stress management techniques.

Taking an active role in self-care is another crucial element of managing chronic illnesses and health conditions. Engaging in regular physical activity, adopting a healthy diet, and getting sufficient rest are all essential aspects of maintaining optimal health. Men over 60 should also prioritize regular check-ups and screenings to catch any potential health issues early on. Staying informed about the latest advancements in medical research and treatments can empower individuals to make informed decisions about their health.

Lastly, it is crucial for men over 60 to recognize and address any mental health challenges that may arise as a result of managing chronic illnesses. Feelings of frustration, sadness, and anxiety are common, and seeking professional help for mental health concerns is just as important as physical healthcare. Engaging in activities that promote mental well-being, such as hobbies, socializing, and mindfulness practices, can also contribute to overall mental health and life satisfaction.

In conclusion, managing chronic illnesses and health conditions is a crucial aspect of men's overall well-being after the age of 60. By establishing a strong support network, seeking professional help, practicing self-care, and addressing mental health concerns, men can effectively navigate the challenges that arise. Taking proactive steps towards managing chronic illnesses and health conditions will not only improve physical health but also contribute to a more fulfilling and satisfying retirement.

Utilizing Healthcare Resources and Services

As men enter their retirement years and cross the threshold of 60, it becomes increasingly important to prioritize their mental health and overall well-being. This subchapter aims to guide men over 60 on how to effectively utilize healthcare resources and services to maintain their mental health and thrive in this new chapter of life.

One of the first steps in ensuring optimal mental health is establishing a strong support system. Men often find solace in the companionship of other like-minded individuals who can relate to their experiences. Joining men's groups or clubs that focus on mental health after 60 can provide a safe space to share concerns, seek advice, and build lasting friendships. These support systems can also help individuals find motivation and purpose, creating a sense of belonging and camaraderie.

Regular medical check-ups are essential for maintaining good health during retirement. As men age, certain health conditions may become more prevalent, such as heart disease, diabetes, or prostate problems. By scheduling regular check-ups with healthcare professionals, any potential issues can be detected early on, enabling prompt treatment and preventive measures. Additionally, healthcare providers can offer valuable advice on leading a healthy lifestyle, including exercise routines, dietary recommendations, and stress management techniques tailored to the unique needs of men over 60.

Mental health should never be overlooked in the pursuit of overall well-being. Seeking professional help from therapists or counselors specializing in men's mental health can be incredibly beneficial. These professionals can provide guidance in managing common challenges faced by men in retirement, such as adjusting to new routines, coping with loss or grief, and maintaining healthy relationships. Therapy sessions can also serve as a space to explore personal goals, rediscover passions, and find renewed meaning and purpose in this new phase of life.

In addition to professional help, staying socially engaged is crucial for mental well-being. Engaging in activities that bring joy and fulfillment can help combat feelings of isolation or boredom. Whether it's pursuing hobbies, volunteering, or participating in community events, these activities provide opportunities for personal growth and connection.

Lastly, it is important for men over 60 to familiarize themselves with available healthcare resources and services. This includes understanding insurance coverage, Medicare benefits, and any additional programs or support systems that may be available to them. This knowledge empowers individuals to make informed decisions about their healthcare and take full advantage of the resources that can enhance their well-being.

By utilizing healthcare resources and services effectively, men over 60 can prioritize their mental health, maintain physical well-being, and embrace this new chapter of life with confidence and resilience. Remember, it's never too late to seek support and make positive changes that contribute to a fulfilling retirement journey.

Planning for Long-Term Care and End-of-Life Decisions

As men over 60, it is crucial to acknowledge the importance of planning for long-term care and end-of-life decisions. While these topics may seem daunting or uncomfortable to think about, being proactive in addressing them can provide peace of mind and ensure that your wishes are respected.

One aspect to consider is long-term care. As we age, the likelihood of needing assistance with daily activities increases. It is essential to plan ahead to ensure that you receive the necessary care and support when the time comes. This can involve exploring options such as in-home care, assisted living communities, or nursing homes. Researching and understanding the costs associated with each option will allow you to make informed decisions that align with your financial situation.

Additionally, it is wise to have conversations with loved ones about your preferences for end-of-life care. These discussions can be difficult, but they are crucial to ensure that your wishes are respected in the event that you are unable to communicate them yourself. Consider documenting your preferences in an advance directive or living will, which can provide guidance to your family and healthcare providers about your desired medical treatments, resuscitation, and organ donation.

Mental health is equally important during this stage of life. Retirement can bring about significant changes, including shifts in social interactions and a loss of identity tied to work. It is essential to prioritize mental well-being and seek support if needed. Connecting with friends and family, engaging in hobbies, and maintaining a healthy lifestyle can all contribute to positive mental health.

Furthermore, it can be helpful to seek professional help or join support groups specifically tailored to men over 60. These resources can provide a safe space to discuss and address common concerns, such as adjusting to retirement, managing relationships, and coping with feelings of isolation or anxiety.

Remember, planning for long-term care and end-of-life decisions is not a sign of weakness but rather a responsible and empowering step towards ensuring your future well-being. By addressing these topics head-on, you can alleviate stress for yourself and your loved ones, allowing you to focus on enjoying this new chapter of life.

Chapter 10: Embracing the Next Chapter

Embracing Change and Embracing Growth

Adjusting to retirement and thriving after 60 can be both exciting and challenging. For many men, retirement marks a significant transition in life that may bring about a mix of emotions. It is essential to recognize that this new chapter can offer immense opportunities for personal growth and fulfillment. In this subchapter, we will explore the importance of embracing change and how it can positively impact men's mental health after 60.

Change is an inevitable part of life, and retirement is a prime example of a significant life change. Instead of viewing retirement as an end, it is crucial to see it as a new beginning. Embracing change means being open to new experiences, ideas, and perspectives. It involves letting go of old routines and embracing the unknown with enthusiasm and curiosity.

Retirement provides the perfect opportunity to reconnect with passions and explore new interests. It is a chance to rediscover oneself and pursue activities that bring joy and fulfillment. Whether it's taking up a new hobby, joining social groups, or learning new skills, embracing change can lead to personal growth and a sense of purpose.

Men over 60 often struggle with mental health issues such as depression, anxiety, and loneliness. Embracing change can significantly impact mental well-being by providing a sense of purpose and belonging. It allows individuals to build new social connections, engage in meaningful activities, and maintain a positive outlook on life.

Furthermore, embracing change can help men develop resilience and adaptability. As we age, we may face various challenges, such as health issues or the loss of loved ones. By embracing change, men can cultivate the ability to navigate these challenges with grace and resilience. It allows them to view setbacks as opportunities for growth and to approach life's ups and downs with a positive mindset.

In conclusion, embracing change is a fundamental aspect of thriving after 60. By embracing this new chapter in life, men can unlock their full potential, find fulfillment, and enhance their mental well-being. Change offers endless possibilities for growth, self-discovery, and personal transformation. It is an invitation to venture into uncharted territories and embrace the gifts that retirement brings. So, men over 60, don't fear change; embrace it and watch your life flourish in ways you never imagined.

Celebrating Achievements and Embracing Life's Possibilities

Subchapter: Celebrating Achievements and Embracing Life's Possibilities

Introduction:
Life after retirement can bring about mixed emotions for men over 60. On one hand, it marks the end of a long and fulfilling career, while on the other, it opens up a world of new possibilities and opportunities. In this subchapter, we will explore the importance of celebrating past achievements and embracing the endless

possibilities that lie ahead. By doing so, we can nurture our mental well-being and ensure a fulfilling and purposeful life after 60.

1. Reflecting on Past Achievements:

As men over 60, it is essential to take the time to reflect on a lifetime of accomplishments. Celebrate the milestones you have achieved throughout your career, personal life, and relationships. Acknowledge your hard work, dedication, and the positive impact you made in your field. This exercise will not only boost your self-esteem but also provide a sense of fulfillment and pride in your past achievements.

2. Transitioning into Retirement:

Retirement marks a significant transition in life, bringing with it a mix of emotions. Embrace this change by focusing on the newfound freedom and the opportunity to pursue passions that may have taken a backseat during your working years. Allow yourself to envision the endless possibilities that lie ahead and the exciting adventures waiting to be explored.

3. Setting New Goals:

Retirement does not mean the end of setting goals; rather, it is an ideal time to set new ones. Consider the areas of life that you wish to improve or explore further. Maybe you want to learn a new skill, travel to new destinations, or engage in volunteer work. By setting new goals, you give yourself a sense of purpose and direction, fueling your mental well-being and overall happiness.

4. Maintaining Mental Health:
Men over 60 often face unique mental health challenges. It is crucial to prioritize self-care and seek support when needed. Engage in activities that bring joy and fulfillment, such as exercise, hobbies, socializing with loved ones, or joining support groups. Remember, it's never too late to start taking care of your mental health and seeking professional help if required.

Conclusion:
As men over 60, we have a wealth of experience and wisdom to draw upon. By celebrating past achievements and embracing life's possibilities, we can embark on a new chapter filled with purpose, fulfillment, and joy. Transitioning into retirement provides an opportunity to redefine ourselves and explore new passions. Let us take charge of our mental health, set new goals, and thrive in this exciting phase of life. Together, we can make the most of the years ahead and create a legacy that inspires future generations.

Creating a Fulfilling and Thriving Retirement Experience

Retirement is often seen as the beginning of a new chapter in life, a time to relax, enjoy hobbies, and spend more time with loved ones. However, for many men over 60, the transition to retirement can bring about a mix of emotions and challenges.

This subchapter aims to guide men through this adjustment period and help them navigate the path to a fulfilling and thriving retirement experience.

One of the key aspects to consider is mental health. Retirement can sometimes lead to feelings of loss, purposelessness, or even depression. It is crucial for men over 60 to pay attention to their mental well-being during this phase of life. Engaging in regular physical activity, maintaining a healthy diet, and seeking social connections are all essential for maintaining positive mental health.

Additionally, seeking professional help or joining support groups specifically tailored to men's mental health can provide invaluable guidance and a safe space to share experiences.

Moreover, finding purpose and meaning in retirement is fundamental for a fulfilling experience. Many men have dedicated a significant portion of their lives to their careers, and suddenly retiring can leave a void. Exploring new interests, volunteering in the community, or pursuing a second career can help fill this void and provide a sense of purpose.

Building and maintaining strong social connections is another vital aspect of a thriving retirement experience. Men over 60 should actively seek out opportunities to connect with others, whether through joining clubs or organizations aligned with their interests, participating in community events, or strengthening relationships with family and friends. These connections can provide emotional support, companionship, and a sense of belonging.

Finally, embracing change and adopting a positive mindset are essential for navigating the retirement years successfully. It is natural to feel a sense of loss or uncertainty during this transition, but viewing retirement as an opportunity for growth, self-discovery, and new experiences can lead to a more fulfilling and thriving retirement. Being open to trying new things, setting goals, and maintaining a flexible attitude can help men over 60 embrace the changes that come with this stage of life.

In conclusion, creating a fulfilling and thriving retirement experience for men over 60 requires attention to mental health, finding purpose, building social connections, and embracing change. By actively engaging in these areas, men can navigate the transition to retirement with confidence and optimism, leading to a rewarding and enjoyable chapter in their lives.

Made in United States
Troutdale, OR
07/06/2024

21062586R00040